The
Map to Life
part 2

...putting the Map into Practice

by

Yogi Sally Ann Slight

ISBN: 978-1910123-331

SAS PUBLISHING

DARTMOUTH

DEVON

With thanks to everyone on Facebook
for their questions.

EMOTIONAL SPIRAL

ASCENDING

Unconditional-Love	100% Integrity
Empathy Forgiveness	Compassion Radiant
Passion Empowerment	Abundance Victor
Generous Outward-Focused	Knowledge Service
Powerful Joy Patient	Freedom Trust
Confidence Positive-Self-Talk	Humility Seek-for-Good
Learning Self-love	Enthusiasm Gratitude
Happiness Security	Worthy Cheerful
Acceptance Belief	Productive Expectation
Playful Positive	Organize Courage
Curiosity Peace	Serene Pleased
Hopefulness	Calm Optimism

Boredom	Boredom
Overwhelm Fear	Jealousy Frustration
Insecurity Pessimism	Judgment Self-pity
Grief Unsupported	Revenge Anger
Failure Hatred	Doubt Depression
Heartache Rejection	Impatience Worry
Depression Disappointment	Negative-Self-Talk
Despair Discouragement	Blame Sorrow
Worthless Humiliation	Irritation Helplessness
Low-Self-Esteem Victim	Bitterness Dread
Unworthiness Shame	Guilt Apathy
No-Will-to-Live	**Death**

DESCENDING

Putting the Map

into the practice

of

your

everyday Happiness.

FEELING LOST...?
You need a Map

...to guide you back
to where you feel comfortable.

And you also need to experience
all levels of Emotion,
to enable comparison
and then choice.

You have a destiny,
when you have a destination.
It's up to you to choose it...
and to enjoy the journey there.

You CAN choose a
Thought / Feeling destination

...and it's easier with a Map!

To change your **ATTITUDE**,
you choose a higher ALTITUDE
of Thought.

It is your low-level Thoughts
that deplete
your physical Energy!

Smile,
to rise upwards again,
into the Thoughts that
refresh,
restore,
and renew
your
Energy.

GRIEF

See where Grief is on the map…
See where Love is…

You feel bad because
you have stayed too long in Grief.
You feel separated
from your loved one because
your Thoughts are so different
than theirs.

Our Thought Energy attracts the same
levels of Energy.
So, be Thankful for all the good times.
Gently, remember the good times.
Gently speak with them,
because they are still with you…
in LOVE.

DEPRESSION

It is impossible to be on
2 different Thought levels at once.

The Thoughts,
that create the feelings of Happiness,
overcome depression.

You create depression,
by staying too long
in the Thoughts down there,
...so, you keep feeling bad.

This is a practice,
that over time,
creates a habit of true Happiness,
that feels so good,
all the time.

LOVE

Just keep smiling,
to stay in Love.

Spring
into the action
of a Peaceful Thought.

Smile, to rise upwards again.

VICTIM

By choosing
a higher level of Thought,
that overcomes the lower levels
of being a Victim,

...you can no longer suffer.

Because it is impossible
to be on 2 levels at once.

Happiness is always with you,
you just didn't know how to get there.

You can overcome suffering,
due to your wanting to feel better,
and by choosing to be in
the higher levels of Thought.

Just like being in a computer game,
you have been trapped
in the level of...

VICTIM

...by not knowing you can leave,
and
how to leave!

The Map will guide you.

Now it will be
YOUR OWN CHOICE
of Thought,
that makes you feel bad
or good.

Smile, to rise upwards again.

GRAVITY

Remember,
there is gravity in Thoughts,
and you will feel bad
down there.

It is easy to feel bad.

You will feel heavy.
You will feel loaded.
You will ruin your day,
Your month,
Your year.

The hard work is to
SMILE.

The hard work is to
use the muscles in your face
to lift the corners
of your mouth.
That action will allow
a momentum of
higher-level Thoughts,
that create the
E-motions that feel good.

When you feel good,
good can come to you.

The healing Energy of Thought

...is LOVE

EMOTIONAL SPIRAL

Energy

Unconditional-Love	100% Integrity
Empathy Forgiveness	Compassion Radiant
Passion Empowerment	Abundance Victor
Generous Outward-Focused	Knowledge Service
Powerful Joy Patient	Freedom Trust
Confidence Positive-Self-Talk	Humility Seek-for-Good
Learning Self-love	Enthusiasm Gratitude
Happiness Security	Worthy Cheerful
Acceptance Belief	Productive Expectation
Playful Positive	Organize Courage
Curiosity Peace	Serene Pleased
Hopefulness	Calm Optimism
Boredom	Boredom
Overwhelm Fear	Jealousy Frustration
Insecurity Pessimism	Judgment Self-pity
Grief Unsupported	Revenge Anger
Failure Hatred	Doubt Depression
Heartache Rejection	Impatience Worry
Depression Disappointment	Negative-Self-Talk
Despair Discouragement	Blame Sorrow
Worthless Humiliation	Irritation Helplessness
Low-Self-Esteem Victim	Bitterness Dread
Unworthiness Shame	Guilt Apathy
No-Will-to-Live	**Death**

lack of energy

DESCENDING

I'm FEELING BORED & TIRED.

"You are doing fantastically well,
because Boredom is higher than Depressed,
where you were yesterday,
so, well done.

Yet, Boredom is still depleting your Energy,
so, Optimism is the next step up for you.
Optimism feels good compared to Boredom.
Optimism sparks that flow of Energy within you.
It's not a huge step,
and can be achieved by being Thankful
for all you have that is good...
your hands, feet, smile, ability and home, clothes etc.
Tiredness, you now know,
comes from always thinking and speaking
about low level Thoughts,
and will pull you down again.

Get into a feeling of Hopefulness by giving Thanks,
for all that you are already satisfied with,
that will bring you more to be Optimistic about.
And congratulations, on the huge leaps you have
already made up into Boredom.
That's something to be Thankful for,
and keep in the good Thoughts by smiling.
Well done."

As soon as you feel bad,
from a Thought...

Exchange that Thought,
for a higher level,
good feeling Thought.

SMILE and think...
a Thankful Thought,
a Happy Thought,
a Peaceful Thought.

To feel good in a Thought,
is to create good.

There is nothing mystical in
Happiness and Enlightenment.

You either are Happy
...or you are not.

Only YOU know what makes YOU Happy,
so be Happy...
if you want to be.

To be Enlightened is...
to know how to create your own
Joy and Happiness,
and
how YOU create your own suffering!

To be Aware that you are thinking,
and creating your own E-motions,
that you will experience in your Life.

You get to any E-motional destination by
thinking, speaking, writing and being
all that makes you Happy...or sad.

A Map just reminds you what direction
your Thoughts and Attitudes
are taking you in.

Where did you learn what you know?
By someone telling you the way it is, or,
by your own Practice from experience?

You can enjoy your Thoughts
that make you Happy...or sad,
as happiness can also be in suffering!

First, harm no one
...including yourself,
by residing in your low-level
or
harmful past Thoughts.

Happiness can be a choice,
that creates a habit.

You can be habitually Happy,
because you stay longer
in the higher levels of Thought Energy,
rather than sinking back down
into the lower levels of Thought.

This process also applies
to being habitually unhappy.

Thankfully,
we now have a Map
to guide us
to our chosen
Emotional destination.

Smile, to rise upwards again.

"Future medicine, will be the medicine of Frequencies."

Albert Einstein

*

How FREQUENTLY
do you visit the
higher FREQUENCIES
of Thought?

...it is the FREQUENCY of the Thought,
that creates the FREQUENCY
of the E-motion.

The longer you stay in the higher
FREQUENCIES,
and the more you
FREQUENT the FREQUENCY,
the more FREQUENCY {Energy},
you receive.

Thought Energy creates your Good Health.

To **OVERCOME ALCOHOL** =
Energy.

Energy overcomes that need.
The higher Energy Thought levels
feel as good as a drink,
and cost nothing.

Excessive drinking of alcohol,
is a habit you created
by changing your opposing Thought.
You used to LOVE...
Then you accepted the gravity
of a lower Thought,
and so,
you sank into the lower levels.

You keep drinking,
because you do not LOVE in Thought.

Your Thoughts heal you...
a Thought can also harm you.

Have a good Thought Day.

A Thought,
is a choice...

when you know
you can choose it.

Now you know!

PEACE
is always with you,
and that IS a promise.

Peace is always there...
You have just found yourself in some
lower Thinking away from Peace
...and so that doesn't feel Peaceful, does it?

Can you see where Peace is?

You can stay there,
if you focus on Peace.
in
Peaceful Thoughts, words and Actions.

You stay in Peace...
because Peace is always there!

Practice SMILING...
to
rise upwards into Peace.

The Action is to move
the muscles on your face.
The Action is to BREATHE in deeply...
SMILING.
The Action is to rise upwards
into Peaceful Thoughts and words again.

The Peace is to FEEL GOOD in Peace.

The Peace is always with you,
and it feels good there.

When you THINK lower than Calm,
you feel uneasy there.

Life is easier with a Map...
to remind you where you left Peace,
because Peace is always with you,
when you choose to be Peaceful.
Smile, and return to the Peacefulness
that you always are.

There, that FEELS GOOD in Peace.

HOW TO KEEP YOUR RELATIONSHIP

To stay together you must Think alike,
just as you did when you first met,
when you loved
everything about each other.

You learn to Think and Learn together,
or
you separate in Thought.

You feel separated already,
because of the levels of difference
of your Thoughts.

You create a physical separation,
by the difference in Thoughts,
that create the words and actions that
are unacceptable to each other.

Having a Map
helps you both see
in what direction
your Thoughts are taking you…

Together
or
apart.

Share your Thoughts
with each other,
and monitor them easily
Together
with a Map.

Love will show you the way.

I like being Righteous...there is healing in being right!

YOU are creating your future,
every second you think!
So, think of what you DO want
in your good life tomorrow…NOW.

There will be no Thoughts of fear,
when you control the mind
to only think of good Thoughts…
that is called, 'Lighting the dark'!

Only YOU know what you really Love.
Think more of what you Love.
Look at pictures of what you Love.
Listen to music that you Love.
Speak words that are good like…
'I AM LOVED' and 'I AM HAPPY'.
Keep smiling.
This may feel like hard work,
but it starts a habit,
and then your habit becomes your character,
and you rise into what you want to be.
Enjoy every moment of your good Thoughts.
You are worth every one of them.

Destiny
is a
destin'ation

...that is easier to find
with a Map

...and a change of feeling,
is a change of destination.

THE LAW OF CAUSE & EFFECT

Your Thoughts create your E-motions.

The 2 sides of Thought
are working together,
to develop your understanding
of their comparison,
by you experiencing the
Effects of the Cause.

The Cause is always the Thought.

Now, you have a Map,
to enable a choice of Cause.

You can either enjoy the Effect...or not!

Stay in LOVE...

by knowing where you are
Emotionally going

...if you don't stay in LOVE!

THE PAST HAS GONE

Yes,
the past has gone.
You can now choose
a good Thought,
and
a Map makes choosing easier.
So, where would you like to be?

The Practice of being
in your chosen Emotions,
creates a habit
for your new Life experiences.

The harm from the past,
has **GONE.**

...phew!

IGNORANCE IS BLISS
What does it really mean?

To **IGNORE** a wrongdoing...
that was either in someone's words,
or, in an action from another.

You remain on a Blissful/Joyful level,
and nothing that anyone says or does will
affect your high level of Emotion.

Let's look at the word...
IGNORANCE is being used
to lower *your* own self-esteem,
rather than its true meaning of...
The Art of Ignoring Another's Behaviour
...to remain in your own Happiness.

To **Ignore** another is to be in control of
your own Emotions,
regardless of what they say or do.

You may find you are in a moment of time
with someone who is not kind.
Know this time will soon pass,
as they too are in the process of
their own Causes & Effects.

You understand that to **ignore** them, is to
remain in the higher levels of your own
Thoughts and feelings,
for your own good health and Happiness,
and you can walk away easily and quickly.

Ignorance is a form of self-Compassion,
It is developed by experience
and your preference for kindness to self.

So, if you are being **Ignored**,
and you are happy, then they do not wish
to know what you know yet.

IGNORANCE; an act of Self-preservation.

When it is said,
'You are in a storm'

...your Emotions are in a turmoil.

The momentum from the flow
of your Energy,
is depleting from the higher
to lower levels of Thought,
because you have accepted something
that Causes you to question
the Truth of your own
Thoughts and feelings.

IGNORE their truth,
until it flows comfortably with your own.

You know your own Truth,
because you feel good in it.

Take your time with all Truth.

You cannot FALL in Love

...because **Love** rises you above all lower Thoughts, and feels so good.

For everyone...
Life has two Learning paths.

Now,
you have chosen the Happiness path,
the higher path,
the Lighter path,
the kinder path,
the path of good experiences.

You have travelled the depression path,
the lower path,
the darker path,
the suffering path,
the path of bad experiences.

You now understand,
the comparison of Thoughts.

**YOU DO NOT HAVE TO RETURN
TO THE LOWER LEVELS.**

You do not have to erase the negative
Thoughts you have had.
All you must do is think
good Thoughts right NOW,
and to *feel good* in those Thoughts.
You will then align yourself
to a higher frequency,
where no negativity exists.

No matter what negatives you have
thought in the past,
whether 10 years ago or 1 minute ago,
NOW is where your power is.

Right now, you can use your
Thought Power and align yourself higher.

When you know this, you can flow
through your life without fear or regrets,
because you can always think
a Good Thought now.

ANGER.

With every negative Thought,
you create another,
and another is attracted to that,
and so, the Thought goes on,
as you are now experiencing.

Well done,
you have Learnt how to be Angry.
The good news is...
You have the experience for comparison.
You just took it too far and got stuck in it!

So, now you can Learn to be **Peaceful**.

Sit, be still and SMILE,
and imagine that SMILE is
deep in your tummy.
FEEL that your tummy can SMILE.
Feel the warmth and comfort of that
SMILE deep in your tummy.

Take your time, as you now
breathe in deeply and slowly.

Breathing, Smiling and feeling good,
deep into your tummy.
You breathe in slowly
and
breathe out slowly.

Not thinking about the doing,
just feeling good in the Peace of breath.

When you sit, be still and SMILE,
you will attract good feeling Thoughts,
that attract other good feeling Thoughts.

Good feeling Thoughts
will bring all the good you need,
and your life will change for the better.

This is the **Peaceful** process.

However deep you are
in your depression...
there is always something
to feel **Pleased** about.

A **Pleasure** will save your Life.

The work is to look for a Pleasure.
The work is to be, do, taste, smell,
touch those **Pleasures**.
The work is to rise out of your pit
into the Pleasure that **Pleases** you,
and you feel Pleased.
How long can you stay up there?
...perhaps you feel **Pleased**
to be depressed,
because it feels better than
guilt or shame.!

Now, you know the way back
to where you really want to be.

Now you know why Jesus said,
'Never worry'.

There is no **Security** in worry.
When you feel Secure,
you cannot worry.

When the mind feels Secure,
from Thoughts of Self-Love and Trust,
your life experiences improve.

Whatever the life situation,
there is something you should know
that you are **Secure** in...

LOVE.

When you feel Impatient...
You have stopped
Learning!

Smile...
and see what you Learnt
from that!

Just by knowing where **JOY** is...
can raise you up and out of Sorrow.

JOY never left you,
You left **JOY**!

The gravity of your Thoughts
keep you down there.
Choose higher level Thoughts
to return to Joy.

Smile...
to change your mind.

Breathe deeply and slowly,
to bring kindness to your
body and mind again.

...don't stay down there too long

GRIEF

When in **Failure**...

You can
FEEL GOOD
at any time,
just by knowing you have
an **Abundance** of anything...
teabags, time, smiles, thoughts...anything.

FEELING GOOD
in
Abundance
creates more
Abundance.

Go there!

You
Forgive
to
FEEL GOOD.

The past has gone,

...it's all good here
NOW!

Choose sides!

...you never feel like a victim, when you choose to be a **Victor**!

FEEL GOOD
by knowing you can change your mind, by staying on the side that feels good!

The past has gone, it's all good here, **NOW**.

See where **Victim** is...

Whatever happened to you,
is just an experience,
and it has gone.
It is over.
It is the past.
It's GONE!

You only stay as a **Victim**
because you speak about it.
You think about it.
You write about what happened.
You discuss it with a consultant.
You look back over it
and wonder why it happened,
and what you could have done differently.
You remain in it.
YOU stay in it.
So, YOU create more of it.

**NOW,
YOU GET TO CHOOSE...**

...to stay on Victim level,
or
to rise upwards into
FORGIVENESS.

FORGIVE yourself,
for not knowing
how to get out of Victim level.

Perhaps you don't want to
FORGIVE anyone now,
as it is a huge leap,
a *Quantum Jump* as it were.

Now you have a Map
you can see where you are,
and where you want to be.

...and,
YOU CAN CHOOSE
a Happy Thought instead
of your Victim thoughts.

To choose a better Thought,
to replace one that feels bad
when you Think like that.

...and the LONGER YOU STAY IN
GOOD THOUGHTS,
the BETTER YOU FEEL.

Yes, it really is that easy!

You change,
when you
CHANGE YOUR MIND.
...and a Map makes choosing
a lot easier to do.

We are all thinking...
All the time.

Now you have a Map,
to enable better choices of Thought.

It's up to you!

Trust
overcomes
all fear...

Go there!

The most important thing for you to know is...

...that it is impossible
to feel bad,
and at the same time
be having good Thoughts,
...that would defy the **Law**.

Because your Thoughts
Cause your feelings.
Your feelings are the
Effects of the Thought.

If you are feeling bad,
it is because you are
thinking Thoughts
that are *making* you
feel bad.

The only way
to consciously deactivate
a Thought,
is to activate another.

In other words,
the only way to deliberately
withdraw your attention
from one Thought,
is to give your attention
to another.

The less you respond to negativity,

the more **Peaceful** your life becomes.

Love is Righteous and so... cannot be left

A Breath of Good Health...

I lost all my friends,
because I went astray,
so, I started to breathe,
my deep fears away.

I had built up pain,
throughout the years,
my negative thoughts,
had brought me to tears.

In loneliness,
I became so low,
and now it's time,
to let you know,
to breathe in shallow,
is like the grave,
so, breathe in deep,
and your life YOU save.

How did I return,
once more to health?

Make new friends,
and retain my wealth?

Well, I deep breathe in,
& 1,2,3,
I brought back,
positivity!

It's so easy,
you can do,
it even when,
you're on the loo.

While in the car,
stuck in a queue,
what better thing,
than be good to YOU!

While sitting down,
or watching telly,
put down that beer,
and fill your belly...

...with cool fresh air,
and with your smile,
you get to live,
that extra mile.

For every breath,
will overthrow,
the dark thoughts and pain,
that brought you low,
that made your friends,
to leave you there,
because you're horrid,
in despair.

Just start with a smile,
and keep your breath flowing,
know that every deep breath,
is a good seed you're sowing.

Breathe in deep,
and then breathe out,
and that circulates,
the blood about.

Push the tummy in,
right to your back,
know nothings left,
within your sack.

Then once again,
push tummy out,
when you breathe in,
and have no doubt,
that doing good,
to your own self,
will bring to you,
good friends and health.

A wealth of health,
and a wealth of **Joy**,
for loving self,
you must employ,
Discipline,
to pave your way,
and do this exercise,
every day.

Because everything changes,
for the good,
when deep breathing in,
is understood.

So, deep breathe your breath,
be a good friend to YOU,
and you'll attract people,
who think like you do!

Peace be with you.

Love from
Yogi Sally Ann Slight

Anytime you feel a bad feeling,
just stop yourself and say:
**'Something is important here, otherwise,
I would not feel bad.
What is it that I want?'**

And then simply turn your attention
to what you do want.

In the moment you turn your attention
to what you want,
the negative Thoughts will stop,
and in the moment
the negative Thought stops,
...the positive Thoughts will begin.

And in that moment,
your feelings will change
from feeling bad...
...to feeling good.

This is the process of
Changing your Mind.

You think about everything,
all the time!

And you can think good Thoughts,
rather than bad Thoughts,
because you cannot be
in 2 Thoughts at once.

So,
think the Thoughts
you would rather experience,
instead.

The Maps will guide you
to your chosen destination.

Smile, to rise upwards again,
and to keep Righteous.

So Thankful for
feeling bad...

That gave me the choice
to feel good again!

So Thankful for
FEELING GOOD...

Now,
I am aware,
I have left bad...
for good!

'Trauma comes back as a reaction, not a memory'.

An Action is also a Thought.

A reAction is to think about
what happened again,
to reLive it,
to reCover it,
to reCeive it again,
perhaps, because someone
reMinded you about it!

Remember, the past has GONE
...and you survived!

Well done.

.

.

You need a Map
to guide you away
from the Thoughts
that harm you,
that reMind you.

Speak, write and think,
only of the good
you have now,
and how good
the future will be for you.

You can now choose...
because you have a Map!

Have a Good Thought Day.

"...LEAD ME NOT INTO TEMPTATION."

What is, TEMPTATION'?

'Temptation' is,
a moment when you are tempted,
to accept or believe in
an opposing Thought.

Temptation will often feel like an upset,
a disturbance of peace,
anger, fear, guilt, confusion, pain,
or dislike of yourself
or someone else...
and that is always a
false or negative emotion.

So, what do you do?

BREATHE...
SLOWLY,

and BREATHE DEEPLY
INTO THE STOMACH AREA
SLOWLY...
RELEASE THE BREATH
DEEPLY FROM THE STOMACH AREA
SLOWLY...
FORCING IN YOUR STOMACH
to REMOVE THE LAST OF THE BREATH.

SLOWLY...repeating this exercise
and FOCUSING ONLY
on the BREATH ENTERING
and LEAVING YOUR BODY.

*...because this is the Action
which eliminates
the reverse momentum of Temptation.*

Then...
AS YOU SLOWLY BREATHE IN,
FEEL THE COOLNESS OF THE AIR

ENTERING THE NASAL PASSAGE
and PAST YOUR THROAT...
FILLING YOUR LUNGS AND CHEST.

ENJOY THE SENSATION OF THE
FULLNESS OF THE LUNGS.
ENJOY THE COOLNESS OF THE BREATH.
ENJOY THE SENSATION OF LIFE.
ENJOY THE GIFT OF LIFE.

When you have Mastered
the Enjoyment of the breath,
then you can insert
THANKSGIVING
into the Mind.

GIVING THANKS FOR THE BREATH.

Thinking..."THANK"
on the INCOMING BREATH...

and thinking..."YOU"
on the RELEASE OF THE BREATH.

SLOWLY...
BREATHING
&
BEING THANKFUL

You return to your Peace of Mind.

...ready to overcome
the next Temptation!

SLOWLY...'Thank'
SLOWLY...'You'

THANK...YOU

Thank you.

ANXIETY AND HOW TO GET OUT OF IT?

Fear is a reversal of Energy flow,
and you feel anxious in any change
that doesn't feel good.

You must step up a few levels in your
emotional consciousness.
The next level up from fear is Desire,
and so, now we find out
what your true Desire is!

What do you want when you sit and wish?

What is the huge dream you have been
thinking about for so many years.?

SIT,
BE STILL
&
THINK ABOUT THAT.

You have then shifted out of fear,
*because you can only think
one Thought at a time.*

You must do the hard work of
thinking about all that you Desire.

Oh, that is far too hard we hear you say.

Yes, you must sit and think about all the
good things you want in your life,
that steps you out of fear and anxiety
straight away.

It is now your choice,
to stick in fear or,
Think about all the good that you want.

Now, be Thankful…
Because you now know you can choose
a new level of emotion,
to get you back to
Happiness and Peace.

# BI-POLAR...
Bi = 2
mental poles.

Just as this planet has 2 poles,
the Arctic and Antarctic,
we also have 2 mental poles,
the higher and the lower,
*...thankfully the weather is better
in our Thoughts.*

A World map will guide you to either pole.

This Thought Map will guide you
back to **Happiness**,
or
further into **Depression**.

Where would you rather be?
Now, you can go there.

Both Maps are helpful to you.

Bi-polar, is a diagnosis...
To inform you that you are experiencing
all the levels of Thought.
You just haven't learnt to choose them yet,
to enable your Emotional self-control.

True Life is the choice of Thought.
Be Thankful for your time in
the comparison of Thought.
You can now choose,
where you would rather Think from.

By your wanting to feel good...or not!

We hope you stay in **Love**.

*(My uncle Eddie Pike, was on the Transglobe
Expedition with Sir Ranulph Fiennes.
They circumnavigated the world visiting both
poles, the Arctic and the Antarctic.
...they know a lot about Polar poles.*

...I know a lot about mental Bi-polar poles).

When you feel good in
Forgiveness,
It is impossible to be in
a lower level of Thought.
...because
You can only think
on one level at a time

...and it feels great in **Forgiveness**!

You **FORGIVE** because YOU feel better,
(YOU HEAL YOURSELF)

...rather than being on a level of hate,
anger, victim etc. that harms YOU!

Remember,
FORGIVENESS is just a word,
that creates feel good feelings in you.
To feel good is to **FORGIVE**.

ATTENTION PLEASE...

Sometimes you justify giving your
attention to something,
...an argument
a sickness, a regret, an anger etc.
because it is true.
You are experiencing it now,
so, it is true, in this moment now.

Yet, just because it is true now,
is not a good reason,
to give it anymore attention,
because anything that you give your
attention to...
becomes true for longer!

A better question is...
"Do I want to experience this anymore?"

THANK...YOU

...Now,
What are you Thankful for?

...Now,
What are you Thankful for?

...Now,
What are you Thankful for?

...Now,
What are you Thankful for?

...Now,
What are you Thankful for?

...Now,
What are you Thankful for?

...Now,
What are you Thankful for?

...Now,
What are you Thankful for?

...Now,
What are you Thankful for?

Thank you.

www.ingramcontent.com/pod-product-compliance
Lightning Source LLC
LaVergne TN
LVHW022325080426
835508LV00013BA/1325